NORTH NORFOLK

WELLS, WALSINGHAM and the BURNHAMS

JOHN CURTIS

Text by Richard Ashby

SALMON

IN
MEMORY OF THE MEN OF
BURNHAM WESTGATE
BURNHAM SUTTON
AND
BURNHAM NORTON
WHO GAVE THEIR LIVES FOR THEIR COUNTRY
IN THE GREAT WAR
1914 — 1919

INTRODUCTION

What a lovely place this is, a place of gentle contrasts. Here are rolling countryside and lonely marshes, a busy port and hidden harbours, a holy land visited by thousands and the birthplace of the nation's hero, Horatio Nelson. Visit Wells in the holiday season and you will find a bustling quayside and holiday resort. Visit Walsingham in the pilgrimage season and the streets will be sweet with incense and thronged with thousands following the procession. But come here out of season, map-read yourself along the minor roads and everything is different. Here is the authentic English countryside in its quiet beauty, the corn waving in the wind, the water lapping at the edge of the quay, the skylark singing in the clear blue sky.

The War Memorial, Burnham Market

This is a place for simple pleasures, for walking and sailing, for watching birds and wildlife, for painting and photography, and for exploring a part of England that is still comparatively unknown.
Those with a religious bent may enjoy visiting the shrines and the wonderful churches. Those who revere more secular men will follow in the footsteps of the hero of Trafalgar or can tour Holkham Hall and learn about its place in the agricultural revolution.
This is a place which nourishes the soul, rests the mind, feeds the imagination and enhances the senses. Visit it and return refreshed and invigorated, thankful that such places still exist in our frenetic world.

Staithe Street, Wells-next-the-Sea
Wells is built on a medieval grid plan with narrow streets running down to the Quay and crossing connecting passages. Many old houses survive in the courts and alleys. Through an arch off Staithe Street is the house of John Fryer, the Sailing Master involved in the infamous mutiny on the 'Bounty'.

The Quay, Wells-next-the-Sea
For most of its long life Wells has been an important port, trading along the east coast of England and across the North Sea, exporting grain, sugar beet and wool and importing coal and potash for fertiliser. The sea once came right up to here but has receded over the centuries as the salt marshes have developed. The reclamation of vast areas of land in the 19th century and the building of the sea wall have left the port at the end of a mile-long channel. Great 19th century granaries and warehouses line the Quay and the nearby streets; one has been converted into a theatre, while others are now residential apartments.

The Buttlands, Wells-next-the-Sea

Usually the name Buttlands derives from the use of an area for archery practice, but here at Wells it refers to the area which was once a 'wasteland'. It is the town's open space, lined with mature trees and surrounded by stately early 19th century houses, many with flat-topped pillared doorways and with delightful names such as 'Stella Maris' and 'The Haven'. There are also two public houses – the Crown Hotel and the Globe Inn. Here the townspeople regularly celebrate with bonfires, carnivals and fetes.

Church of St Nicholas, Wells-next-the-Sea

The original church was almost entirely destroyed by fire in 1879 after being struck by lightning and was rebuilt in 1883. It contains a 17th century parish chest which still carries the marks of burning. John Fryer of the 'Bounty' is buried in the churchyard, but his gravestone is now safely protected inside the church.

The Harbour, Wells-next-the-Sea

As well as the seaborne trade Wells' prosperity was founded on fishing. Whelks were harvested from the local whelk beds, cooked in great coppers in sheds on the quay and taken away by the harbour railway. Sprats, prawns and whelks are still landed here. Fishing is still important, but now it is leisure sailing which forms the bulk of the activity in the harbour.

Beach Huts, Wells-next-the-Sea

Wells' lovely beach is a mile walk, drive or narrow-gauge train ride from the town along the sea wall. Here is the lifeboat station, and the National Coastwatch lookout station keeps watch over the fine sandy beach fringed by pine woods and dunes. Behind the dunes is a recreational area known as 'Abraham's Bosom', which contains the only salt-water lake in the country. In recent years beach huts have become very desirable property. They are the static successors to the 'bathing machines' of Regency and Victorian times which were drawn into the sea so that bathers could change and then bathe modestly, out of view of the people on the beach.

Holkham Hall

This great 18th century house was built for Thomas Coke, Earl of Leicester, who had been on the Grand Tour to Italy and had returned full of ideas about what a great country house should be.
He worked with William Kent, the architect and landscape designer, and the result is one of the finest Palladian mansions in England. Thomas' heir, known as 'Coke of Norfolk', was a great agricultural reformer and claimed that when he first knew the Holkham estate it was so infertile that two rabbits would be seen fighting over one blade of grass. By the beginning of the 19th century Holkham was famous nation-wide for its progressive farming methods.

Holkham Beach

The vast beach, backed by sand dunes, is part of a National Nature Reserve and home to many different birds. Much of the land behind has been reclaimed from the sea over the centuries by the Cokes of Holkham. The Peddars Way passes along the beach and the final scene of the film 'Shakespeare in Love' was filmed here.

The 'Lord Nelson', Burnham Thorpe
Known as 'Nelson's local', this 17th century pub was certainly visited by the great man. It retains much of its historic atmosphere with open fires, stone flagged floors and traditional wooden settles. The pub serves fine food and 'Nelson's Blood', a blend of rum and spices, which is made to a secret recipe on the premises.

Church of All Saints, Burnham Thorpe
The great English Admiral, the hero of the battle of Trafalgar, was born in the now demolished rectory, nearby, and was baptised in the Church. Nelson loved the village, which he referred to as 'Dear old Burnham', and he returned here after the peace of 1797, when many naval officers were laid off on half pay. Nelson's rector father is buried in the chancel of the church and the Admiral himself wanted to be buried here, but a grateful nation demanded that he rest in St Paul's Cathedral in London instead. The wood of the crucifix on the rood and the lectern are from HMS Victory and there are crests and flags from HMS Nelson presented by the Admiralty.

Burnham Overy Staithe

The River Burn was once tidal as far as South Creake, and in the 13th century, sea-going vessels could navigate as far as Burnham Thorpe, three miles from the sea. The continuous silting of the river gradually drove the trade northwards until only Burnham Overy Staithe was accessible. Nevertheless, the port was busy until the 19th century and the commercial trade only ended in 1920 when it eventually went elsewhere. Today it is a centre for sailing and a base from which to explore the marshes with their extensive bird life.

Burnham Overy Watermill

In 1789 Edmund Savory built a bridge to carry the coast road across the River Burn. A year later he altered the course of the river and built a watermill adjacent to the bridge. The complex eventually included a granary and maltings, a blacksmith's shop, and stables, cow sheds and cottages for the mill and farm workers.

Burnham Overy Windmill
Like many Norfolk mills this is a brick tower mill. It was built by Edmund Savory in 1816 and was worked in conjunction with his nearby watermill. It ceased working in 1919 and after being sold in 1926 the machinery was removed and it was converted into a house.

Church of St Clement, Burnham Overy
This characterful church, with its central tower, has seen many changes over the centuries. It was once a simple Norman structure, but is much altered. The tower may date from Saxon times, but at sometime it has been reduced in height and a distinctive wooden cupola added.

High Street, Burnham Market

The Ordnance Survey map shows seven villages with 'Burnham' incorporated into their name. The three Burnham communities of Sutton, Ulph and Westgate had separate identities and three churches until the 18th century when that at Burnham Sutton was demolished by the Rector, Lord Nelson's father. By the 19th century it was one village and the railway company gave it the name Burnham Market when a station was built here in 1866. With its wide main street lined with 18th century houses, it has been described as 'Norfolk's loveliest village'. It seems to have escaped some of the problems experienced by other villages in the area and still has over forty privately owned shops serving the needs of a wide area.

Church of St Mary, Burnham Market

The village still has two churches and St Mary's, Burnham Westgate has a particularly fine position overlooking the village green. The 14th century tower is surmounted by 15th century battlements adorned with carved biblical and Christian scenes, which include Adam and Eve, Doubting Thomas, Thomas à Becket and a headless John the Baptist.

Friary, Burnham Norton
The Carmelites, or White Friars, established their first house on Mount Carmel after the 12th Century Crusades. Burnham Norton Friary was the first to be founded in England in 1241 by returning Carmelites after the Holy Land was lost. There were never more than 15 friars and only four were left when the Friary was dissolved in 1538.

Church of St Margaret, Burnham Norton
Churches with round towers are rare in most of England. In Norfolk and Suffolk, though, there are some one hundred and seventy-five surviving from Saxon and Norman times, and one hundred and twenty of these are in Norfolk. It was thought that the towers were built round as a defence against Viking invaders, but it is more likely that the lack of local building stone meant that it was easier and cheaper to build a tower in the local flint without using stone blocks for the corners. Inside St Margaret's are wonderful things: a great square Norman font, a painted 'wine glass' pulpit dating from 1450, fragments of medieval wall paintings and a screen on which the painted panels have been defaced and covered over with biblical quotations.

Brancaster Beach
The Roman fort, of Branodonum, nearby, guarded the crossing to Lincolnshire and was part of the defences against the Saxons. Across the inlet are the dunes and salt marshes of Scolt Head Island, famous for its birdlife, including its breeding colony of terns.

Brancaster Staithe
This was once a busy little port and a centre for the fishing industry where sea trout, mackerel and turbot were caught. Oysters were reared here and shell fish harvested from the sea bed. The local pub, 'The Jolly Sailor', has a brewery attached.

Thornham Creek

On a bright summer day the marshes are silent except for the sound of the wind in the rigging of the sailing boats and the skylarks high above children catching crabs in the nearby sluice. Holme Dene Nature Reserve is one of the most beautiful on the North Norfolk coast and home to some very rare endangered wildlife species.

Creake Abbey

It started life as a small hospital and almshouse for the poor. By 1206 there was a church attached and it was known as 'St Mary of the Meadows next to Burnham'. It had become a priory of Augustinian canons in 1230, although there were never more than seven canons in residence at one time. After a fire in 1484 there was not enough money to restore the whole church and the nave and transepts were demolished. Plague finally claimed the lives of all the canons and the sole survivor, the Abbot, died in 1506. The Abbey thus ceased to exist some thirty years before the Dissolution, which destroyed so many others.

Church of St Edmund, Egmere

It is not certain why this church and its surrounding medieval village were abandoned. It has been suggested that the village was a casualty of the Black Death which laid waste to the population of England, but the church was a dependency of the Priory at Walsingham and may well have suffered when that was dissolved and its assets sold.

Church of St Mary, South Creake

With its many altars, statues and shrines, medieval glass, 15th century screen and the absence of fixed pews, entering this church is to step back into pre-Reformation times. There is a wonderful carved and painted roof which celebrates the Battle of Agincourt. Its angels hold the arms of the Black Prince, musical instruments and the symbols of Christ's Passion.

**Shrine of Our Lady of Walsingham
Little Walsingham**
Walsingham has been a centre of Pilgrimage
for nearly a thousand years. In the 1920s, the
Vicar of Little Walsingham had a replica of
the Holy Statue carved, which was initially
placed in the Parish Church, but then, in 1931,
transferred to a rebuilt 'Holy House', around
which has grown this shrine church.

Common Place, Little Walsingham
The village grew up around the great
Priory in order to serve the needs of the
pilgrims, and there were hostelries for
their accommodation as well as a great
range of trades and services. The
destruction of the Priory must have
devastated the village and destroyed
the very reason for its existence.
Perhaps it is because of this that so
many late medieval and 17th century
buildings still survive, since there was
no reason to develop and build new.
The revival of the shrine and the
re-establishment of pilgrimage again
draw many thousands each year and,
once more, many buildings are given
over to their accommodation and care.

Slipper Chapel, Houghton St Giles
In 1062, the Lady Richelde was commanded in a vision to build a replica of the 'Holy House' of Nazareth. This shrine, enclosed in a chapel and then a great church built by Augustinian Canons, became the object of many pilgrimages and second only to the shrine of Thomas à Becket at Canterbury. Its royal patrons included Henry III and Edward I. Henry VIII came here and gave a valuable necklace to the statue, but it was he who later ordered its destruction. It was customary for pilgrims to walk the last mile barefoot and here at this little chapel in Houghton St Giles they took off their shoes. It is now the centre for Roman Catholic pilgrimages.

Priory ruins, Little Walsingham
Of the splendours which must have been, only this archway and window, ruins of the east end of the great priory church, now remain. The gardens, which are open to the public through the Shirehall Museum, are peaceful most of the year but at Pilgrimage time are thronged with thousands for the special services held here.

Priory Gatehouse, Little Walsingham

Perhaps most impressive of all is this great gatehouse, which formed the entrance to the Priory from the High Street. The pilgrims passed beneath the gate, into the sacred precincts, and though the church to the Holy House where they worshiped before the statue of Our Lady of Walsingham, the climax of their long and arduous journey.

Published and Printed in Great Britain by
J. Salmon Ltd., Sevenoaks, Kent TN13 1BB. © 2007
Website: www.jsalmon.com. Telephone: 01732 452381.
Email: enquiries@jsalmon.co.uk.

Design by John Curtis. Text and photographs © John Curtis.

Photographs pages ten and thirty by kind permission of
Holkham Hall and Walsingham Abbey.

ISBN 1-84640-098-8
Title page photograph: Cottage at Great Walsingham.
Front cover photograph: The Quay, Wells-Next-The-Sea.
Back cover photograph: Cottage at Burnham Overy.

Salmon Books
ENGLISH IMAGES SERIES
Photography by John Curtis

Titles available in this series

English Abbeys and Priories

English Gardens

English Country Towns

English Cottages

English Landscape Gardens

English Follies

English Villages

English Country Pubs

English Castles

English Cathedrals

English Country Churches

Jane Austen's England

Romantic England

Mysterious England